GW00976496

TO

FROM

THE BOSS:
NAMELESS, BLAMELESS, AND SHAMELESS

A DILBERT® BOOK
BY
SCOTT ADAMS

The Ink Group

ISBN: 1 876277 40 8

http://www.inkgroup.com

The Ink Group Pty Ltd Publishers
Sydney, Australia 2015

The Ink Group Publishers Limited
Swindon, Wiltshire SN5 7TH England

The Ink Group NZ Limited
Albany, Auckland, New Zealand

THE BOSS:
NAMELESS, BLAMELESS, AND SHAMELESS

THE COMPANY IS A BILLION DOLLARS BELOW ITS EARNINGS PROJECTIONS.

FROM NOW ON, ONLY THE MANAGERS AT MY LEVEL OR ABOVE MAY EAT DONUTS AT COMPANY MEETINGS.

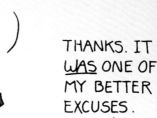

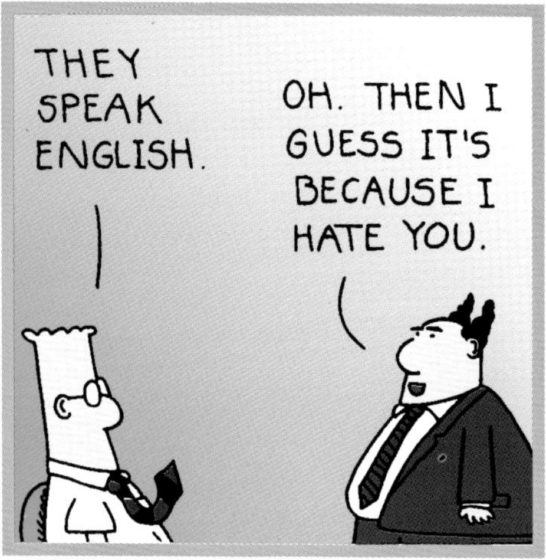
THEY SPEAK ENGLISH.
OH. THEN I GUESS IT'S BECAUSE I HATE YOU.

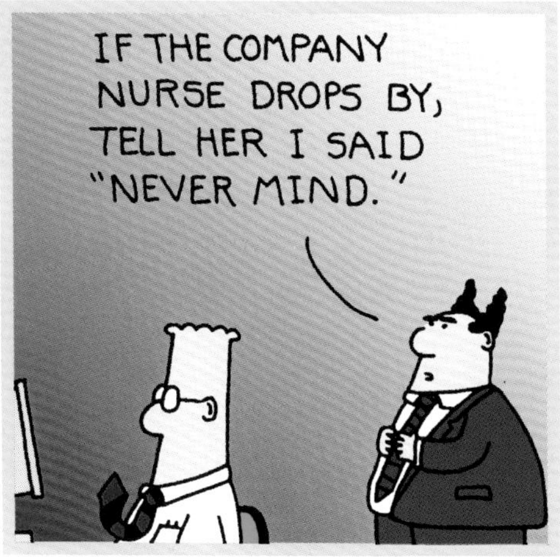
IF THE COMPANY NURSE DROPS BY, TELL HER I SAID "NEVER MIND."

HOW LONG DOES THE TRANQUIL-IZER LAST?
HE'LL WAKE UP AT THE UNEMPLOY-MENT OFFICE.

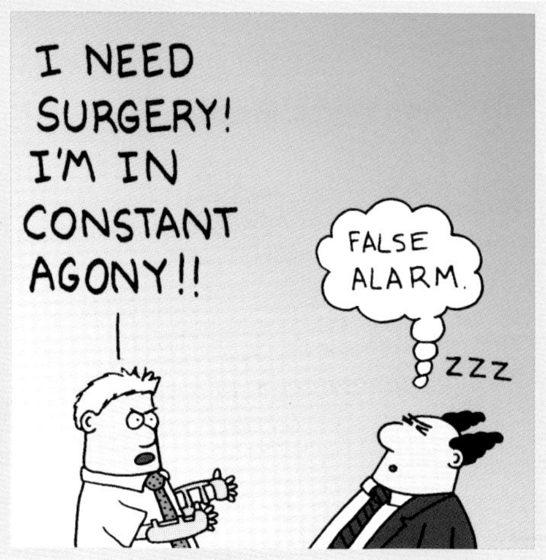
I NEED SURGERY! I'M IN CONSTANT AGONY!!
FALSE ALARM.
ZZZ

RUN AND GET ME SOME PAPER TOWELS... FIVE OF THEM... FROM THE MEN'S ROOM.
WHAP!

THAT'S NOT EXACTLY THE POINT.
I SAW "THE CRYING GAME." DON'T DO ANYTHING THAT WOULD MAKE ME HEAVE.